CANADA'S ARCTIC ANIMALS

Chelsea Dona

Scholastic Canada Ltd.

Toronto New York London Auckland Sydney
Mexico City New Delhi Hong Kong Buenos Aires

Scholastic Canada Ltd.
175 Hillmount Road, Markham, Ontario L6C 1Z7, Canada

Scholastic Inc.
555 Broadway, New York, NY 10012, USA

Scholastic Australia Pty Limited
PO Box 579, Gosford, NSW 2250, Australia

Scholastic New Zealand Limited
Private Bag 94407, Greenmount, Auckland, New Zealand

Scholastic Ltd.
Villiers House, Clarendon Avenue, Leamington Spa,
Warwickshire CV32 5PR, UK

Every reasonable effort has been made to trace the ownership of copyright material used in the text.
The publisher would be pleased to know of any errors or omissions.

Visual Credits

Cover, p. i (border), p. iii (border): © Steve Bloom Images/Alamy; p. i, p. 14, p. 18: W. Lynch/Ivy Images;
p. iv (map): Hothouse Canada; pp. iv–1 (Arctic scene): NOAA, Dept. of Commerce/Rear Admiral Harley
D. Nygren (ret.); p. 2, p. 5: F. Bruemmer/Ivy Images; p. 3: © Doug Allan/www.naturepl.com; p. 4, p. 22,
p. 44 (caribou & polar bears): Alaska Division of Tourism via SODA; p. 6: Rinie Van Muers/
Foto Natura/Minden Pictures; p. 8: Daniel J. Cox/www.naturalexposures.com; p. 9: W. Lankinen/
Ivy Images; p. 10: Daniel A. Bedell/Maxximages.com; p. 11, p. 20: Bill Lowry/Ivy Images; p. 12, p. 41,
p. 43: Flip Nicklin/Minden Pictures; p. 13, p. 24, pp. 24–25: Michio Hoshino/Minden Pictures; p. 15:
© Johnny Johnson/DRK Photo; p. 16: Thomas Kitchin & Victoria Hurst/firstlight.ca; p. 17: Johnny
Johnson/Maxximages.com; p. 19: Jim Brandenburg/Minden Pictures; p. 21: Parks Canada/
W. Lynch/13.02.10.01(136); p. 23, p. 27, pp. 28–29: D. Taylor/Ivy Images; p. 26: W. Towriss/
Ivy Images; p. 30: © Robert E. Mumford Jr./Natural Images Photography; p. 31: Office of NOAA
Corps Operations; pp. 32–33: Len Lee Rue III/Ivy Images; pp. 34–35: Brian Milne/Maxximages.com;
pp. 36–37, pp. 38–39, p. 40: Dr. Chris Harvey-Clark, University of British Columbia; p. 44
(Arctic tern): Dr. Bill Freedman, Dalhousie University

Produced by Focus Strategic Communications Inc.
Project Management and Editorial: Adrianna Edwards
Design and Layout: Lisa Platt
Photo Research: Elizabeth Kelly
Consultant: Hugh Gabriel Shaftoe

Special thanks to Dr. Chris Harvey-Clark of the University of British Columbia
and Dr. Bill Freedman of Dalhousie University for their expertise.

Library and Archives Canada Cataloguing in Publication
Donaldson, Chelsea, 1959-
Canada's arctic animals / Chelsea Donaldson.
(Canada close up)
ISBN 0-439-95673-0
1. Animals--Canada, Northern--Juvenile literature. 2. Animals--Arctic regions--
Juvenile literature. I. Title. II. Series: Canada close up (Markham, Ont.)
QL105.D65 2005   j591.75'86'09719   C2005-901030-4

6 5 4 3 2 1   Printed in Canada   05 06 07 08 09

TABLE OF CONTENTS

Welcome to the Arctic!   **1**

CHAPTER 1:   **Seal**   **2**

CHAPTER 2:   **Polar Bear**   **7**

CHAPTER 3:   **Arctic Fox**   **13**

CHAPTER 4:   **Arctic Hare**   **18**

CHAPTER 5:   **Caribou**   **22**

CHAPTER 6:   **Arctic Tern**   **27**

CHAPTER 7:   **Walrus**   **31**

CHAPTER 8:   **Greenland Shark**   **36**

CHAPTER 9:   **Narwhal**   **41**

The Canadian Arctic

North Pole

Arctic

Arctic Circle

Alaska

Canada

United States

Canada

Arctic

Arctic Canada

United States

Welcome to the Arctic!

The Arctic is the area around the North Pole. It is the coldest place in Canada. In fact, it is one of the coldest places on Earth.

In some parts, small plants grow for a few weeks in summer. This area is called the Arctic tundra. Other parts stay frozen all year round. They are permanently covered with a thick layer of ice called a glacier.

It is not easy for animals to stay alive in the Arctic. Animals that live here must know how to find food and keep warm.

Let's meet some of these clever creatures.

CHAPTER ONE

Seal

Did you know that dogs are not the only animals that bark? Seals bark, too. They sound a little like a dog with a sore throat! Dogs and seals may sound alike, but they don't have very much else in common.

Seals are part of the *pinniped* (PIN-i-ped) family. Pinniped means that they have fins, or flippers, for feet. Seals use their flippers for walking and swimming.

The most common type of seal in the Canadian Arctic is the ringed seal.
Its name comes from the pattern of rings on its fur.

Ringed seals spend a lot of time under the ice. They swim in the cold Arctic water. But, like all seals, they need to come up for air.

They must dig breathing holes. Ringed seals are very good at this. They dig through the ice with their claws.

Baby ringed seals are usually born in late winter. The mother seal builds a den inside a snowdrift. From the outside, no one can tell the seals are there.

The secret den is built above a breathing hole in the ice. The hole gives mother and baby a quick way out. You never know when a hungry polar bear will come calling!

The hooded seal is another kind of Arctic seal. The male hooded seal has a special trick. It can blow up a sac on top of its nose. The sac looks just like a black balloon!
It can also blow a red balloon out one nostril.

We're not sure why the male seal has these two balloons. It may use them to give warning, or even to attract females during the mating season.

CHAPTER TWO

Polar Bear

A polar bear sits very still beside an ice hole.
It sits so still, it looks like a lump of ice.

A big seal pokes its head out of the water.
Quickly, the bear grabs the seal's head in
its sharp teeth and powerful claws.
It pulls the seal out of the water.

The seal struggles to get free. Then it
stops moving.

The bear carries the dead seal to its den.
It is a mother bear, and she shares the
seal with her two hungry cubs. The seal
blubber will feed them all for a few days.

Seal is the polar bear's favourite food. But bears will also hunt animals such as walrus, reindeer, sea birds and fish. They sometimes even kill and eat beluga whales.

When food is hard to find, bears eat eggs and berries. If they are very hungry, they will also eat garbage.

Polar bears are huge! When they stand on their hind legs, they are taller than the tallest person you know. Full-grown males can weigh up to 780 kilograms. That is about as much as ten men.

A polar bear's coat has two layers. The bottom layer, close to its skin, is made of thick, waterproof fur. On top of this fur is a thinner layer of stiff, shiny hairs. The hairs are actually clear. They only look white or yellow when light hits them at a certain angle.

Polar bears also have a thick layer of fat under their skin to keep them warm. These layers of fur and fat work so well that polar bears often get too warm!

What do polar bears do when they get hot? The same thing we do. They go swimming.

Polar bears are great swimmers. They can swim 100 kilometres using their front feet as paddles. They can dive down to chase seals or to get around an ice floe. Bears can stay underwater for up to two minutes.

How long can you hold your breath?

CHAPTER THREE

Arctic Fox

Polar bears usually hunt alone. But they often have company. Arctic foxes will follow a bear to grab any leftover meat.

But the foxes have to be careful. They don't want to become the bear's next meal!

The Arctic fox and the polar bear share something else. They are both hard to spot against the white snow.

In winter, the fox's white coat helps it to sneak up on its prey. In summer, the coat will turn brown or grey. It blends in with the tundra. Some Arctic foxes have fur that looks blue!

Arctic foxes live in dens. Sometimes they dig dens into hillsides. Sometimes they make dens along riverbanks. Sometimes their dens are in piles of large rocks.

Foxes live in family groups, but two or more families might join together. In winter, they dig tunnels through the snow to connect their dens.

Males and females usually stay together after mating. They both look after their young.

Young foxes are called kits. There are usually six to eight kits in a litter. But sometimes there are more. One mother fox had a litter of 25 kits!

Young foxes have big appetites. Feeding them can be a lot of work. When foxes aren't following bears to get food, they hunt small animals, such as lemmings.

Lemmings are furry animals that look a bit like mice. Older fox kits can eat about ten lemmings a day!

CHAPTER FOUR

Arctic Hare

Another animal that foxes like to eat is the Arctic hare.

The Arctic hare is hard to spot. Like the fox and many other animals, it changes colour from season to season.

Usually, the Arctic hare is white. But in summer, its coat turns brown or blue-grey, like the tundra. Only its tail stays white all year round. Changing colour helps the hare hide from its enemies.

Hares also hide by sitting very still. Baby hares are called leverets. They can sit very still by the time they are three days old. They look like small brown rocks.

Sometimes, a fox or other predator will see the hare. Then the hare has to get away — *fast*. It may run away on all fours. Or, it may hop on its hind legs, like a kangaroo.

An Arctic hare can run more than 60 kilometres an hour. That's as fast as a car in the city!

When it's being chased, it zigzags across the tundra. That makes it hard for its enemies to catch it.

Arctic hares have strong claws to help them dig for food. They eat bark, twigs, berries, leaves, roots and mosses. They even eat seaweed.

Their sharp noses help them smell food beneath the snow. If the snow is too crusty, they will gnaw it with their teeth or thump it with their feet to break it.

CHAPTER FIVE

Caribou

Have you ever looked at the back of a quarter? The animal you see there is a caribou.

Caribou are big animals. But they are also very quick. Some caribou can run as fast as a car. Even a baby caribou can run faster than a person by the time it is a day old!

Caribou are easy to recognize because both males and females have antlers. But male antlers are much bigger. All caribou shed and regrow their antlers every year.

Males use their antlers to fight each other. They lock their antlers together. Then they wrestle to see who will win. The winner of the fight gets to choose a female to mate with.

Baby caribou are born in June. They are called calves. They grow quickly over the summer. The calves eat as much as they can so they will be strong and healthy by the fall.

Caribou must keep moving to find food. They feed on small plants and grasses that grow on the tundra. When the weather gets colder, they travel south.

Large herds of caribou follow the same routes every year. But not all of them survive the journey.

Wolves also know the caribou routes. They attack the herd. They kill the weakest and slowest animals.

The wolves kill the caribou for food. But they also help the caribou herd to survive. If some of the caribou did not die, the herd might not have enough food to last the winter.

CHAPTER SIX

Arctic Tern

The Arctic tern is another animal that goes south for the winter. Every fall, terns fly to the Antarctic, near the South Pole. When it is winter in the Arctic, it is summer in the Antarctic. By flying south, these birds enjoy summer all year round.

Arctic terns fly thousands of kilometres to reach the Antarctic. This may be the longest migration of any animal in the world!

Arctic terns live together in colonies.
Sometimes a colony has only a few birds.
Sometimes it has thousands.

It can be a very noisy place! Terns do not
twitter or sing. They screech.
PI-PI-PI-PI-PI. KEE-AW! KEE-AW!

When a predator threatens a member of
the colony, the whole colony attacks.
They dive at the intruder's head to scare
it away.

It's fall, and it's getting cold.
Suddenly, the whole colony of
screeching birds goes quiet.
Then, all together, the birds
rise up into the sky.

What an amazing sight!
The Arctic terns have begun
their long journey south.

CHAPTER SEVEN

Walrus

Walrus are odd-looking creatures. They
have small heads. They have whiskers
around their noses. They have flippers
instead of hands or feet. And their bodies
are covered by a thick layer of fat.

Walrus are big and clumsy
on land. Their odd shape
makes it hard for them to
move across the ice. Even so,
they can move faster than a
person over short distances.

But in the water, walrus are not clumsy
at all. In fact, they are very graceful.
Their small heads help them glide
through the water. Their whiskers help
them to find food. Their flippers help
them to swim fast. And the layers of fat
keep them warm.

Walrus can even sleep in the water!
Because of the way walrus are shaped,
their heads naturally float on the water.
Also, air sacs in their necks act like
life jackets.

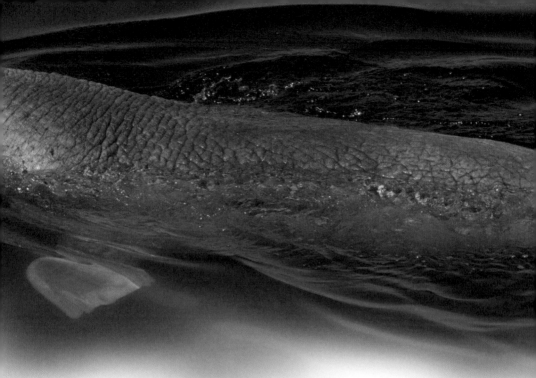

What other odd feature do walrus have?
Big, long front teeth, of course! These are
called tusks. Walrus tusks can be up to a
metre long. Imagine if *your* front teeth
were that big.

Walrus use their tusks to pull themselves
up onto the ice or dig for food under water.
Male walrus sometimes use them to fight.
But mostly, they use them to show off!
The walrus with the longest tusks is usually
the most important walrus in the group.

Did you know that walrus can change colour? When the water is very cold, they are almost white. In warm weather, they can turn pink or even red because of algae that grows on their skin. But most of the time they are brown.

When a walrus is hungry, it dives to the sea bottom. It uses its nose and whiskers to find food. It digs in the sand for clams and snails. A walrus has a split upper lip. This helps it suck a clam right out of its shell. One walrus can eat up to 6000 clams at a time.

Walrus also use a neat trick to get food. They take a big mouthful of water. Then they blow it out at the sand. The jet of water uncovers animals hiding on the ocean floor. Snack time!

CHAPTER EIGHT

Greenland Shark

In the darkness,
deep,
    deep,
        deep
below the surface of the Arctic Ocean,
a giant waits. It hardly moves. It has
rows and rows of short, sharp teeth.
Its cloudy white eyes almost seem to glow.

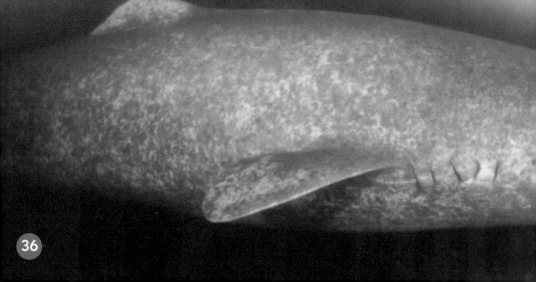

A fish swims toward the giant. SWOOSH! In a second, it is pulled into the giant's mouth. CHOMP!

The Greenland shark's eyes do not really glow. They only seem to glow because they reflect light. The odd colour comes from a small animal called a *copepod* (KO-pi-pod). The copepod attaches itself to the shark's eye. It makes the shark blind.

Being blind does not really bother the shark. It uses its senses of smell, hearing and touch to hunt. And the copepod hanging from its eye may help to attract fish.

The Greenland shark is also
called the sleeper shark. That's
because it spends a lot of
time not moving.

Scientists think that it does
not need to chase after its dinner.
It waits for dinner to come to it. When
fish swim close by, the Greenland shark
sucks water into its mouth like a vacuum.
All of the nearby fish get pulled in as well.

Greenland sharks also eat seals,
beluga whales and even other sharks.
Sometimes whole caribou are found in
the stomachs of Greenland sharks!
But no one knows if they hunt prey or
eat only dead creatures.

A Greenland shark is huge. But it grows
very slowly. An adult shark grows only
about one centimetre a year. So a big
adult could be hundreds of years old!

These sharks are so big, they don't have
many enemies. Even people don't eat
them very much. Their flesh is poisonous.
It has to be boiled or dried before it can
be eaten.

CHAPTER NINE

Narwhal

Have you ever seen a unicorn? Of course you haven't! Unicorns exist only in fairy tales.

But there is an animal with a horn like a unicorn. It is called a narwhal. A narwhal is a type of whale that lives in the Arctic.

Narwhals have very few teeth. When a male narwhal is about two years old, its upper left tooth begins to grow straight out. As it grows, it twists around and around. It looks just like a unicorn's horn.

Sometimes two of the male's teeth will grow into horns. And sometimes even a female will grow a horn. But no one is really sure what the horn is for.

Some people think male narwhals fight with them. Males often have scars that could have come from fighting. Others think they use the horn to attract mates. Or maybe they use the horn just to show off.

Narwhals are almost as hard to find as unicorns. That's because they are very shy. So we do not know much about them.

One thing we do know is that they like to chat! When they talk, narwhals make a lot of different noises. They WHISTLE. They CLICK. They SQUEAL. What do you think they are saying?

The Arctic creatures you have read about are all one-of-a-kind. Each has found its own ways to survive.

They are all tough Arctic animals!